GARNET
HAZARD

Canadian Christmas

WATERCOLOR

GARNET HAZARD

CHRISTMAS

An American Annual of Christmas Literature and Art

Edited by Randolph E. Haugan

Volume Forty-Four

Augsburg Publishing House · Publishers · Minneapolis

Volume Forty-four

Second Edition

Nineteen Hundred Seventy-four

Acknowledgments

THE CHRISTMAS STORY 5–13
Illustrations by Conrad Pickel, courtesy of Conrad Pickel Studios, New Berlin, Wisconsin.

GLORIA 45
Poem reprinted from *In the Rustling Grass*, copyright © 1964 Augsburg Publishing House.

THE GENTLE LIGHTS OF CHRISTMAS 46–47
Photos courtesy of New Mexico Department of Development.

CHRISTMAS MUSIC 54–60
Calligraphy by Hildegard Szendrey.

THE ART OF FEEDING WINTER BIRDS 65–67
Reprinted from *The Minnesota Volunteer*, November–December 1973.

Photos by Marjorie Carr, Duluth, Minn., and Norman Kordell, Afton, Minn.

The Cardinals in Snow are by Albert Earl Gilbert, one of America's leading wildlife artists. The original painting was published in full color print form in 1973 by the National Wildlife Art Exchange, Inc., P.O. Drawer 3385 — Suite 3, Vero Beach, Fla. 32960. The prints are suitable for framing, hand numbered, signed by the artist and published in a Guaranteed Limited Edition of 1500. The painting and prints were © copyrighted by the National Wildlife Art Exchange, Inc. in 1973 — ALL RIGHTS RESERVED and is reprinted with the express written permission of the Exchange. The original painting was donated to the Commonwealth of Kentucky and presently hangs in the Governor's Office.

LAYOUT AND DESIGN: GEORGE NORDWALL

POETRY EDITOR: MELVA ROREM

MUSIC EDITOR: RUTH OLSON

THE CHRISTMAS STORY

According to St. Luke and St. Matthew

Illustrated by Conrad Pickel

AND IT CAME TO PASS in those days, that there went out a decree from Caesar Augustus, that all the world should be taxed. (And this taxing was first made when Cyrenius was governor of Syria.) And all went to be taxed, every one into his own city. And Joseph also went up from Galilee, out of the city of Nazareth, into Judea, unto the city of David, which is called Bethlehem, (because he was of the house and lineage of David,) to be taxed with Mary his espoused wife, being great with child. And so it was, that, while they were there, the days were accomplished that she should be delivered. And she brought forth her firstborn son, and wrapped him in swaddling clothes, and laid him in a manger; because there was no room for them in the inn. And there were in the same country shepherds abiding in the field, keeping watch over their flock by night. And, lo, the angel of the Lord came upon them, and the glory of the Lord shone round about them; and they were sore afraid.

THERE WERE SHEPHERDS IN THE FIELD

AND THE ANGEL
said unto them, Fear not: for, behold, I bring you good tidings of great joy, which shall be to all people. For unto you is born this day in the city of David a Saviour, which is Christ the Lord. And this shall be a sign unto you; Ye shall find the babe wrapped in swaddling clothes, lying in a manger. And suddenly there was with the angel a multitude of the heavenly host praising God, and saying, Glory to God in the highest, and on earth peace, good will toward men. And it came to pass, as the angels were gone away from them into heaven, the shepherds said one to another, Let us now go even unto Bethlehem, and see this thing which is come to pass, which the Lord hath made known unto us. And they came with haste, and found Mary and Joseph, and the babe lying in a manger. And when they had seen it, they made known abroad the saying which was told them concerning this child. And all they that heard it wondered at those things which were told them by the shepherds. But Mary kept all these things, and pondered them in her heart. And the shepherds returned, glorifying and praising God for all the things that they had heard and seen, as it was told unto them.

THEY FOUND MARY AND JOSEPH AND THE BABE

**ow when Jesus** was born in Bethlehem of Judea in the days of Herod the king, behold, there came wise men from the east to Jerusalem, saying, Where is he that is born King of the Jews? for we have seen his star in the east, and are come to worship him. When Herod the king had heard these things, he was troubled, and all Jerusalem with him. And when he had gathered all the chief priests and scribes of the people together, he demanded of them where Christ should be born. And they said unto him, In Bethlehem of Judea: for thus it is written by the prophet, And thou Bethlehem, in the land of Juda, art not the least among the princes of Juda: for out of thee shall come a Governor, that shall rule my people Israel. Then Herod, when he had privily called the wise men, inquired of them diligently what time the star appeared. And he sent them to Bethlehem, and said, Go and search diligently for the young child; and when ye have found him, bring me word again, that I may come and worship him also. When they had heard the king, they departed; and lo, the star, which they saw in the east, went before them, till it came and stood over where the young child was. When they saw the star, they rejoiced with exceeding great joy. And when they were come into the house, they saw the young child with Mary his mother, and fell down, and worshipped him: and when they had opened their treasures, they presented unto him gifts; gold, and frankincense, and myrrh. And being warned of God in a dream that they should not return to Herod, they departed into their own country another way.

THERE CAME WISE MEN FROM THE EAST

AND WHEN THEY WERE departed, behold, the angel of the Lord appeareth to Joseph in a dream, saying, Arise, and take the young child and his mother, and flee into Egypt, and be thou there until I bring thee word: for Herod will seek the young child to destroy him. When he arose, he took the young child and his mother by night, and departed into Egypt: And was there until the death of Herod: that it might be fulfilled which was spoken of the Lord by the prophet, saying, Out of Egypt, have I called my son. . . . But when Herod was dead, behold, an angel of the Lord appeareth in a dream to Joseph in Egypt, saying, Arise, and take the young child and his mother, and go into the land of Israel: for they are dead which sought the young child's life. And he arose, and took the young child and his mother, and came into the land of Israel. But when he heard that Archelaus did reign in Judea in the room of his father Herod, he was afraid to go thither: notwithstanding, being warned of God in a dream, he turned aside into the parts of Galilee: And he came and dwelt in a city called Nazareth: that it might be fulfilled which was spoken by the prophets, He shall be called a Nazarene.

THE FLIGHT INTO EGYPT

The
Holy
Family

Michelangelo

Michelangelo: Giant Among Men

JEAN LOUISE SMITH

HE WALKED tall. He associated with princes and popes. Yet his life style was so simple that he was sometimes mistaken for a pauper. Michelangelo Buonarroti was his name; sculptor, painter, architect, and poet, he was a giant among men.

Michelangelo was born 500 years ago on March 6, 1475, in the tiny mountain village of Caprese in Italy. His father was Lodovico Buonarroti, mayor of the village, and his mother, Francesca di Neri di Miniato del Sera. Shortly after Michelangelo's birth the family moved to Florence, and his mother, unable to nurse her child, found a stonecutter's wife to wet-nurse the tiny baby. For more than six years this kindly peasant woman looked after the foster child who grew sturdy and healthy under her care. Three more sons were born to Michelangelo's real mother before she died, and although the widowed father remarried shortly, he felt that Michelangelo would do better in a good grammar school than in his overcrowded home. And so the boy was sent off to boarding school at an unusually early age.

Michelangelo's teachers complained that he spent far more time making sketches than studying the prescribed subjects. The complaints mounted over the years, and reports of the young student's work became so poor that his despairing father finally gave in to his son's pleadings to be allowed to study art.

Michelangelo was enrolled in the large and important workshop of the painter Ghirlandaio. Amid the smell and sight of paint, Michelangelo found inviting canvases to be covered and enthusiastic and talented art students to talk with. He began to find himself, and he became an eager art student. For several months he was content to learn all he could from his renowned and talented teacher. Ghirlandaio was a respected figure in the city of Florence, and important families kept him busy with commissions for portraits and frescoes.

When Michelangelo was enrolled in this studio, Ghirlandaio was working on a series of frescoes for the walls of the Church of Santa Maria Novella—an extensive project that required the assistance of several artists. In all probability young Michelangelo was

15

CARRARA—*Noted for its quarries. Here Michelangelo selected blocks of fine marble. These he carved into notable sculptures such as his "David," his "Moses," and the "Pietà" for St. Peter's.*

BOLOGNA—*Here, Michelangelo, at age twenty, carved his "Kneeling Angel" and two other figures for the tomb of St. Dominic.*

CARRARA   BOLOGNA

FLORENCE—*City of the Medicis, ruled by Lorenzo de Medici—Later by Savonarola. Here Michelangelo developed from a protégé of the Medicis to full stature as a sculptor and painter. Here he created "David," his "Doni Pietà," the Medici Tomb, and his "Pietà" for St. Peter's. He served as architect for the Florence Cathedral dome, and for San Lorenzo Church.*

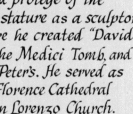

FLORENCE

CAPRESE

CAPRESE—*The birthplace of Michelangelo—March 6, 1475. His father, Lodovico Buonarroti, soon moved his family from this tiny village back to Florence where they had lived previously.*

LORENZO de MEDICI   SAVONAROLA

ROME

PIETA

ROME—*Site of Michelangelo's renowned "Pietà" in St. Peter's and the multi-figured tomb of Julius II, with its powerful figure of "Moses." As an architect he created St. Peter's dome and the Roman Civic Center. As a painter he created the notable Sistine Chapel ceiling and his "Last Judgment."*

•NAPLES

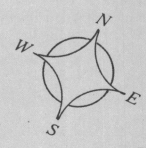

JULIUS II   ST. PETER'S   Da VINCI

N
W   E
S

one of them. At any rate, during the three years that he spent with Ghirlandaio, he moved from the mundane work of mixing pigments and cleaning brushes to the important tasks of making large cartoons from small drawings, and preparing plaster for his teacher's frescoes and doing minor work on them. He learned about form, style, line, and color, both in the studio and from careful observation as he went daily to see what the masters of art had done or were doing in the art-minded city of Florence. Most often he went to the Church of the Carmine to study Masaccio's frescoes. He made many drawings of the figures, for they were remarkably rounded and had such true form that it seemed as though they might come alive and walk about in the atmosphere which Masaccio had created for their setting.

The sight of these forms made Michelangelo want to experiment with stone and marble sculpturing during the hours when he was not painting. Just as Masaccio had seemed to form his figures so that they took on rounded shapes and became like real bodies of bone and flesh, Michelangelo was able to do sculptured figures as though they were released from the bondage of marble.

Lorenzo dé Medici, patron of the arts and a member of the wealthy and politically powerful Medici family, was a frequent visitor to Ghirlandaio's studio. Michelangelo had been an apprentice in the workshop for nearly three years when Lorenzo began to take special notice of him. One day he paused longer than usual to look over the young artist's shoulder. For some time he had been thinking of inviting him to study art with several of his protégés and stay in the palace of the Medici. After Lorenzo asked Michelangelo if he would like to do this, he accepted the offer eagerly, especially since Lorenzo was quite agreeable that he study sculpture. Lorenzo treated him like a son, giving him fine clothes and a generous allowance.

This move was a turning point, for now Michelangelo was free to study the art he loved best in an atmosphere that was alive with talk of art, poetry, philosophy, and politics. As a patron of the arts, the Medici family welcomed the leading persons in these fields to the palace, where they mingled with the art students; they admired and discussed the many works of art which made the palace like an art museum.

Sixteen-year-old Michelangelo took it all in! This stimulating experience came to a sudden end with the death of Lorenzo, for Piero dé Medici, his son and successor, was pleasure-loving and not particularly art-minded. In fact, his taste was so poor that the Florentines shortly dubbed him "Piero, the Unfortunate." The only thing he asked Michelangelo to do was to make a statue in snow. Insulted and frustrated, Michelangelo made the statue and immediately packed his equipment and left the palace for his father's home across the city near the Church of Santa Croce.

Then followed 10 years of silence—years about which very little is known of either his life or work.

Jeremiah—*Vault of the Sistine Chapel*—1510

Behold, the days are coming, says the Lord, when I will raise up for David a righteous branch, and he shall reign as king.
Jeremiah 23:5

His known labors during this period consisted of a wooden crucifix for Santo Spirito and three small statues. Yet, Michelangelo undoubtedly worked at his art, for a great talent like his never remains inactive.

The city of Florence was literally crowded with splendid examples of art from ancient times to Michelangelo's own day, which was at the very peak of the Renaissance. It is more than likely that Michelangelo used much of his time during those 10 silent years to study the frescoes and paintings of men like Fra Filippo Lippi, Leonardo da Vinci, Gozzoli, and sculptors such as Donatello and Ghiberti. In San Marco, close to where he lived with his family, he could see frescoes by Fra Angelico depicting the life of Francis of Assisi. As he looked at these works of art he probably made sketches that helped him understand the techniques of these great men. This was something that his teacher, Ghirlandaio, had considered a valuable exercise.

Two unrelated happenings influenced young Michelangelo during those years: the preaching of Savonarola, the "rebel monk," and visits to Carrara where Italy's finest marble was quarried.

The journey to Carrara from Florence would have taken a day or so, and the young sculptor would have lingered long to watch the skilled laborers cut the marble blocks and slabs. Perhaps he would lend a hand himself. In any event, when commissions for sculpture began to come, Michelangelo was well prepared to choose marble that would be exactly right. He liked to select the marble himself. From those

Moses—1513-1516

early visits to Carrara, he knew that the marble had to be split along a fault. He would search for marble that had fault-lines spaced so that the block, when cut, would be the size he needed. He would watch while the workmen forced olive wood wedges into the fault-lines and then poured water onto the wood. The water expanded the wood, and the marble would split neatly along the fault. Anxiously, Michelangelo would watch while the blocks were hauled on to rollers and eased down chutes or slides with rope and tackle. If the marble block broke loose, it would more than likely be ruined. And so those early visits to watch the proceedings at Carrara were of life-long importance to Michelangelo.

Also of significance was the fiery preaching of the monk, Savonarola. Michelangelo, a devout and believing Christian, listened attentively to Savonarola's pleas for reform within the church. Much later in life, when he painted the "Last Judgment" over the altar in the Sistine Chapel, the figures of the blessed and the condemned in that fresco were vividly reminiscent of Savonarola's preaching and pronouncements about the fate of men who chose good or evil as a way of life.

When Michelangelo was 21 years old, he went to Rome to see the wonders of antiquity—those marvelous sculptures and architectural ruins that were to exert a great influence on his style. He stayed in Rome for four years, absorbing all that he could of the ancient art. Back in Florence, he began to receive commissions once more from the Medici family. They had decided that they must have a splendid tomb, worthy of their rank in life. They exerted influence on Pope Julius II to commission such a tomb, and Michelangelo submitted the plan that the pope and the Medici liked best. Michelangelo was told to go ahead with his grandiose plan for the family tomb. Although he worked on it for 40 years, he never really finished it. He was not able to start the seated figure of Pope Julius II, and he managed to do only a few of the 40 statues and many reliefs that he planned. A good part of the difficulty came because the pope would frequently demand that Michelangelo leave the work on the tomb to undertake other assignments. This frustration proved to be the trial of Michelangelo's long life. Nonetheless, he was able to complete the monumental statues of "Day" and "Night," "Twilight" and "Dawn." He made numerous trips to Carrara to supervise the selection and cutting of the marble, which had to be in very large blocks for such heroic-sized figures.

There were other practical problems: funding was one, for when the temperamental pope would not send money, Michelangelo was unable to pay for marble or labor, and of course he had no money for himself. Experiences like this forced him to live and work like a common laborer—a circumstance that in time became a style of life for him. He never bothered with more than enough money to barely survive.

The time came when the work on the tomb had slowed down to the point that Michelangelo needed to find other work, and he accepted a commission to do the facade of the Church of San Lorenzo in Florence. After devoting three years to this, the whole project was suddenly canceled. The dejected Michelangelo wrote a friend, "I am *ruined!*" But it was not long before he was called to resume work on the Medici tomb.

After some delay in getting the right marble, Michelangelo received a message from the pope that he had been selected as the artist best suited to decorate the Sistine Chapel. In genuine distress he objected, "I am a sculptor, not a painter!" But his protests went unheeded. The pope was firm.

Reluctantly, Michelangelo erected the scaffolding in the chapel so that he could paint the ceiling and the upper areas of the walls—curved spaces between windows which proved to be most difficult to paint. Actually, he had done very little painting since he had left Ghirlandaio's studio. Botticelli, Perugino, Signorelli and Ghirlandaio—all important artists of the day—had created frescoes for the walls of the chapel. Raphael was to do a series of tapestries later on. Michel-

THE SISTINE CHAPEL

angelo's paintings on the ceiling and arched spaces were to begin with the story of creation and end with the fall of man. In all, he planned 343 colossal figures to tell the various epic stories. Each episode was sketched and then transferred to a full-size cartoon before he could begin to paint.

Michelangelo told the story of creation from the book of Genesis. In bold, sculpture-like forms, he pictured the creation of the world, the sun, moon, and growing things, of Adam and Eve, of the temptation, the flood. He pictured God as a person—a majestic figure with a great cloak enveloping and supporting him like a cloud, spinning the earth with a magnificent gesture. He reaches out and touches Adam so that he may rise from his pre-existent sleep.

In the triangular spaces between the windows, Michelangelo chose to picture Old Testament prophets—all strong and vital men. He showed them brooding, or as though on fire with the message of the coming One. To these men, he added adjacent figures of several sibyls, women who prophesied with pre-Christian insight the coming of a messiah.

Month after month, Michelangelo labored on the ceiling. "I am growing a goiter," he wrote his family, describing how he had to lie on his back and strain his neck and arms into unnatural positions for this difficult task. Sixteen months passed and he had covered less than half of the ceiling and the triangular spaces. The pope became angry and urged him to speed his work.

The statue of Lorenzo dé Medici, often called "The Thinker."

It was another 12 months before the ceiling was done and the scaffolding could be taken down. This allowed him to work on the curved spaces, the lunettes —the most difficult task of all. In four years, minus a few weeks, the unveiling took place. On All Saints' Day, October 31, 1512, the chapel was opened for the curious and eager crowds to see the work that had taken so long to do. They looked in awe at what must have seemed like a magnificent unfolding of the stories of creation. They saw a veritable procession of seven Old Testament prophets who foretold the coming of Christ: Zechariah, Joel, Isaiah, Ezekiel, Daniel, Jeremiah, and Jonah. Years later, the "Last Judgment" was to fill the end wall behind the altar, but for now the Old Testament personages were enough; indeed, they must have been overwhelming.

This accomplished, Michelangelo turned again to work on the Medici tomb. He did exactly three statues before the project was again called off for a time, for the pope wanted him to do more work on the facade for the Church of San Lorenzo in Florence. Michelangelo set to work on the project at once, and drew up a plan which called for 12 very large statues and several smaller works as well. Immediately after the plan was approved, he began the sculpturing. Before many months had passed, he was summoned to Rome and told that he had been chosen to be the chief architect for the new St. Peter's Cathedral. Fortunately, this was a task that was very much to his liking. Furthermore, Pope Paul III gave him full authority to plan and carry out the project. Michelangelo decided to do the dome himself. He made it 404 feet above the street level—the highest yet designed.

The work on St. Peter's went slowly. Michelangelo spent one year alone making a model, which can still be seen in St. Peter's.

One would think that the pope would protect Michelangelo from interruptions while engaged in so important a task as St. Peter's, but, unbelievably, he was asked to design a staircase for the reading room of the Laurentian Library in Florence. The actual construction of the project was left to others who followed Michelangelo's model. The staircase was a most unusual structure which is frequently described as being like a stream that broadens as it flows. Others compare the staircase to music; still others speak of it as being like a flow of lava. Perhaps these are all different ways of trying to describe a structure that seems to move and flow with great beauty and dignity. For 500 years, learned men have mounted and descended this staircase, remembering the great mind that designed it.

Michelangelo was not to see the completion of St. Peter's, nor did he live to finish the Medici tomb or the facade of San Lorenzo. It would seem as though here was a man who apparently had no qualms about planning work and signing contracts that were altogether too vast for one human being to complete within a lifetime. He was one who was so possessed by an

Pieta—1498

all-enveloping and consuming genius that it seemed as though he was forced to run to keep up with it!

Not all of Michelangelo's works were as overpowering and epic in nature as the Sistine Chapel and the Medici tomb. As a young man, he had several important commissions for single works. Some of these are well known and greatly loved, the "Pieta" being one. This beautiful sculptured piece, known to many in America because it was once on loan to a world's fair, was executed in 1498 on commission from a French cardinal, Jean Bilheres de Lagraulas, who wanted it for a chapel in Old St. Peter's in Rome. The way that Michelangelo showed the body of the dead Christ lying across Mary's knees created considerable technical difficulties, since the smaller form of the woman had to support the larger male figure. He solved the problem by raising Mary's right knee to support and raise the long male body. Mary's gesture, as she extends her left arm over the body, speaks eloquently of her personal sorrow.

Michelangelo chiseled his name on Mary's shoulder strap—the only work he ever signed.

The "Pieta" was done in Rome, and when it was completed Michelangelo went to Florence where he was asked by the Doni family to paint a holy family. Since he had been studying and working fairly recently in Ghirlandaio's workshop, it was not difficult for him to turn again to painting. Actually, the "Doni Madonna" is a kind of sculpturesque painting, with well-rounded, massive three-dimensional figures which make it difficult to believe that they are on a flat surface. The choice of a *tondo*, or circular form, challenged the ingenuity of the artist to the difficult task of placing four figures within a circle. He solved this problem by curving and twisting the bodies so that the child Jesus stands on Mary's shoulder, and Joseph bends over them. The infant John is close by, and behind, leaning against a wall, are a number of young men. A theological interpretation of this holy family is that here is a symbolizing of the lifting up

21

Self portrait

of the Child in the presence of paganism, which is represented by the youth. Another interpretation is that the youth (who seem to be disrobing) symbolize persons getting ready for John to baptize them. Regardless of how one chooses to interpret the painting, it is a serious and thought-provoking piece. Clear blue and rich shades of red and gold are the dominating colors—blue for faith, and red for sacrifice and humanity.

In 1504, the year after Michelangelo completed the Doni painting, he received two commissions from the Pitti and the Taddei families. Both were sculptured madonnas done in fairly low relief. The "Pitti Madonna" shows a quietly composed Mary who sits relaxed as her child rests against her. The young John can be seen in the background looking over Mary's right shoulder.

In a more active mood, the "Taddei Madonna" pictures the child Jesus turning hurriedly to his mother, perhaps in fear because John is offering him a goldfinch. In art, the goldfinch symbolizes the passion of Christ, since that bird eats thorny foliage.

From everything we know about Michelangelo, the man and his works, he emerges as a giant—a special kind of giant. One of his contemporaries described him as ugly, having a huge head with a forehead that seemed almost square. His ears were large and flat, and he had a crooked nose which had been broken during an argument with another sculptor. His eyes were fiercely piercing. His medium-sized body seemed almost too frail to support the broad shoulders and large head.

Michelangelo was a lonely man who was so thoroughly submerged in his work that even his closest friends had difficulty getting to him. Not so his family! Frequently in debt, the brothers made demands for money and support for themselves and their father. Michelangelo never turned his family down, no matter how difficult they made life for him.

He had few friends. His only woman friend, whom he first knew at about age 60, was Vittoria Colona, a widow who came from a high-born family. Theirs was a platonic friendship which lasted 13 years, until her death. Vittoria had a fine mind; she was sympathetic in her understanding of Michelangelo's problems, and, like him she wrote poetry.

As Michelangelo aged, his isolation from people became more marked. At 75, ill health and poor vision began to make it difficult for him to work—yet he did, right up to his death. He spent most of his time alone, living in poverty that was not necessary but which he had assumed from an early age.

Following a stroke in 1563, he was able to accept a peaceful attitude toward himself and his work. In 1564—the year of his death—he dictated his will, leaving his soul to God, his body to the earth, and belongings to nearest relatives. Early one raw February morning he went for a walk. Friends who saw him realized that he was wandering about quite confused. They took him home and called the two doctors who had been looking after him. His friends gathered around him and on February 18, 1564, he died. His body lay in state in the Church of the Holy Apostles in Rome, and it was there that he was buried.

Artist friends in Florence, hearing of his death but not knowing that the funeral had taken place, hurried to Rome to claim his body. They knew that Michelangelo had always counted Florence as his real home, and that he had spoken of wanting to be buried there. When his family and friends discovered that Michelangelo was already buried, they stole the body and took it to Florence to the Church of Santa Croce. When word spread among the people that their beloved sculptor had been brought home, a great crowd gathered in the church and demanded that the lid be taken off the coffin so that they could look again at their friend.

Several artists asked Vasari—Michelangelo's friend, and an artist—to design a tomb. On it were three mourning figures representing sculpture, painting, and architecture—the three arts to which Michelangelo had given all of his life. In July, after the tomb was finished, a memorial service was held in the Church of San Lorenzo. Michelangelo's body finally came to rest in his beloved Church of Santa Croce.

Looking back over the 500 years since Michelangelo's birth, the world of culture and of art continues to acclaim him as a giant among men. Acknowledged as a genius in his own day, the master's work has stood all of the tests of time. His name comes often to people's minds and lips as one who is a kind of universal man. The manner in which much of the world was outraged over the mutilation of his "Pieta" in 1972, testified that Michelangelo and his art belong to our day as much as to his own time.

Madonna of the Stairs—about 1491

Michelangelo was one who believed that an individual's life always should be consistent with his religious beliefs. This meant for him, that as one who portrayed the Old and New Testaments, he should lead a blameless life. He was a man who prayed; he was forgiving, generous, and faithful to all whom he served as well as to members of his family and his friends. His integration of personality and Christian commitment resulted in the kind of art that communicates divine love.

In 1555, nine years before his death, Michelangelo wrote a sonnet which sums up his philosophy of life. Translated by the English poet, William Wordsworth, it reads:

The prayers I make will then be sweet indeed
If Thou the spirit give by which I pray:
My unassisted heart is barren clay;
That of its native self can nothing feed:
Of good and pious works Thou art the seed,
That quickens only where Thou say'st it may:
Unless Thou shew to us thine own true way
No man can find it: Father! Thou must lead.
Do Thou, then, breathe those thoughts into my mind
By which such virtue may in me be bred
That in thy holy footsteps I may tread;
The fetters of my tongue do Thou unbind,
That I may have the power to sing of Thee,
And sound thy praises everlastingly.

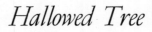

Mary, Remembering

I hold it close against my heart—that night
In little Bethlehem, so long ago.
I still can sense the hush and see the glow
Of silent stars that shed a mystic light,
And hear the winter wind that was so bold.
Joseph was desperate when he found no room.
A stable offered shelter from the gloom
And cold, where sheep dozed in the quiet fold.

And then the Baby's cry. . . . The world stood still
The moment when I looked upon the Child
And saw how fair of face he was and mild,
While angel music drifted from the hill.
Heaven was round me and the holy One
That star-lit hour I held God's precious Son.

WILLIAM ARNETTE WOFFORD

Hallowed Tree

"Look," you said,
*   breaking the silence*
*   of September woods.*
"That maple
*   is a Christmas tree!*
*   Each leaf has a red border—*
*   red and green*
*   with the sun for tinsel."*

Alone,
*   this Christmas Day,*
*   that memory*
*   will grace my room—*
*   "red and green*
*   with the sun for tinsel"*
*   and the thought of you*
*   its halo of lights.*

MYRA SCOVEL

Poems of Christmas

To Every Purpose There Will Be a Time

There would not be another day before
The journey. Time was gone and time was near
And Mary was afraid. She found no peace
In one more day of rest. In fading light
She sat, absorbing every precious view
Of pillar, floor, and roof, of lamp at dusk.
And would she miss the hammer's fall, the smell
Of pine, the sight of olive slopes beyond
The wall? Far back in Mary's mind there was
The faintest prodding of the words that she
Had heard so long ago: Fear not.
But for these words the days could not accept
The miracle within, the song with pain,
The joy with weariness. The day was gone.
She rose to light the lamp, but did not hear
The jackals' wail beyond the fields of flax,
The evening cry of hunger from the hills,
She only heard the steps of Joseph near.

HAZEL FORD

Yggdrasil*: A Christmas Vision

Once, long ago, upon a cedared hill
high-summer-smelling in a grey December
my father and I were searching for a tree,
the perfect tree in a great world-grove of cedar.
I liked them all, they were all green and friendly,
alive with sap and fragrance and casual prickles.
We took the right one home in the Model T.
The children (I was nine and one of three)
Lit glowing candles like rapt acolytes;
they were the real thing, these colored fires
dancing perilously upon the green branches,
scenting the scene with austere fragrance of flame.
The tree was dressed in gold and silver tinsel,
with frankincense and myrrh, and filled the room
and suddenly the room with light and color.
It was the world, a radiant thing, a marvel,
a world burning to a starry apocalypse,
from the top of the tree to the top of heaven shining.
—I am haunted by that simple cedared epiphany,
the fabled East endenizened in the West,
the homely prickly feel of the living green,
The sticky gold dust clinging to my fingers.
I lie under, and look, a lost child,
and find the tree enrooted in my heart.
It is there forever, a creation of earth and heaven,
immortal Yggdrasil, dying and ever green.

LAWRENCE G. NELSON

* The mystical tree in Scandinavian mythology that overspreads
  the world and binds earth, hell, and heaven together.

24

Home for Christmas

RUTH L. DIEFFENBACHER

HOME means many different things to as many different people, but at no time more than at Christmas does each of us long for and strive to go home, wherever it may be.

It was in 1823 that Henry Rowley Bishop's opera *Clari, or The Maid of Milan,* was first heard in London. The music was Bishop's, but the text was partially written by John Howard Payne—words which have been sung by succeeding generations.

John Howard Payne had roamed through the palaces of Europe and savored their pleasures, but his words were wrung from an inner loneliness.

> 'Mid pleasures and palaces
>> though we may roam,
> Be it ever so humble,
>> there's no place like home.

Amid the glitter of Europe's capitols, Payne longed for the little cottage at East Hampton, Long Island, New York. That cottage with its white picket fence and windmill in the side yard was home. Perhaps it was Christmas when those words were penned, and Payne was seeing in his mind's eye the drifts of snow and the frosted and iced grasses at the edge of the grey winter waters of the Atlantic.

This same urge drove our ancestors to push across the country with rumbling wheels and creaking harnesses. Sometimes home was a lumbering prairie schooner with a swinging Advent wreath. Sometimes it was a sunbaked adobe on the southwestern desert or a chinked log cabin in the depths of the forest. Sometimes it was a homesteader's sod hut. Whether western ranch, New England cottage buried in drifts of snow, or elegant eastern townhouse, it still was home and the place to be at Christmas.

In those early days of our country, home was where the family settled. And sometimes, in order to carve out a home in the wilderness, sons and daughters had to leave the old home and push on in wagons and schooners into the unknown, untried, and at times hostile territory. Yet at Christmas the old traditions were observed and cherished. The well-remembered and well-loved customs were kept alive: the tree was cut and trimmed, the carols were sung, and the stockings were hung by the fire. Cherished memories warmed the hearts of those who were far from home.

As our country grew, the old trails and early coach routes gave way to canals, riverboats, and a network of railroads stretching from shore to shore. They made a Christmas journey back to the old home place possible.

So the annual trek began. We have always been a nation on the move, but never so much as at Christmas. Today our roads are choked with an endless stream of traffic, and our airports are filled with jostling, milling crowds. It seems that the whole world is going home for Christmas.

Although Christmas is a family time, perhaps it would be well to contemplate the lonely people who no longer have family or home or those who, through circumstances which they cannot control, are unable to get home. Some of us learned in this past year what the crisis of imposed travel restrictions could do to our Christmas plans.

Although there have been deprivations and disappointments, our separations were not as acute as in the past when war separated loved ones. Soldiers lived with their memories and their hopes for happier Christmases back home.

Mary and Joseph were forced to be away from their home when Jesus was born. It had been a long and tiresome journey—well over 150 miles from Nazareth to Bethlehem. It must have taken a long time with Joseph walking beside Mary, riding on that donkey. And the weariness and concern grew when there was no room at the inn. But his little family made a home in a stable, and they cradled their babe in a manger.

Gilbert Chesterton said it well with his words:

> Only where He was homeless
> Are you and I at home.

The circular courtyard of Baltimore's Old Colony Inn, much like an old English inn, was flooded with arriving and departing guests. The air was alive with a festive holiday spirit. Inside the inn, fires glowed and fiddles played rollicking tunes as the departing guests trooped down the staircase.

"One more cup of hot tea before we face that cold ride," cried Henry.

"No, Henry, there isn't time," insisted Sally Lou as she gathered up her skirts to avoid the snow which dusted the path to the coach.

The whip sat atop the drag and adjusted his riding

apron over his knees while the groom held the horses in check. Some of these travelers had come from Philadelphia and were all too ready for what the inn could offer in the way of rest and refreshment. Others were on their way to Annapolis to attend the Governor's Christmas Ball. It seemed that everyone was making a journey to be with old friends at Christmas.

"Step lively; we have no time to dally," cried the impatient groom. There were happy calls of greeting and farewell, and exchanges of "Merry Christmas" rang out in the frosty air while the carolers who had gathered around the tree added their holiday wish.

The horses had to be shod, and that required a trip into town to the blacksmith. Katrina and her brother John had begged to ride along in the bobsled. Now, while they were removing the harness, Katrina could savor all the activity of this booming Kansas town.

After the vast open spaces of their prairie farm, this looked like a metropolis. Cowboys on horseback were in town to shop for supplies. The overland coach was drawn up under the frosted elms in front of the hotel. A family was boarding the coach for a Christmas trip.

Cutters and prairie schooners and even an old Conestoga wagon filled the streets, and the air rang with the clamor of Christmas preparation.

Snow powdered her bonnet as a boy nearly John's age pushed the snow off the blacksmith's shop roof.

"How exciting," breathed Katrina. "All these people so busy going and coming! I can feel Christmas in the air." This town was certainly the place to see everything and to catch the holiday spirit. "I'll have so much to tell everyone when we get back home."

"Hello there," called the friendly engineer. Mary and Eric waved back in joyous greeting. They were bursting with anticipation; they could hardly contain themselves. Going to Chicago to spend the holidays with their grandparents was certainly exciting. But they would have the added thrill of riding on this train. Father had promised that they would sleep in the Pullman and eat in the dining car.

This was a great Christmas for the children's parents too. Amanda's family had expressed their reserva-

tions when she had gone west with her husband. Ranching was hard work; the unsettled west had been rough and difficult. But the years had brought success, and now they were going back east with a trunk full of fine clothes and lovely gifts. The gift for Amanda's mother was so fragile that she insisted upon carrying it in her own hands.

Soon the baggage would be loaded in the baggage car, and they would be on their way home for a memorable Christmas.

"Did you ever see so many people on the streets as there are today? My word, everybody is in such a hurry. That store was a nightmare. But now we've finished our shopping, and we can go home and trim our tree."

Elsie and Bud sloshed along in their arctics, determined to leave the hustle and bustle of the city behind them. Only a few hours before the train would arrive! There was the tree to trim and the last wrapping to be done before they would meet their parents who were

coming from Pennsylvania to spend Christmas with them.

Children hurried through the streets, clutching skates, skis, or a sled. Others lingered in the snow, patching a snowman or discussing a hockey game.

The noisy street cars, honking horns, and hurrying crowds were rather tiring. "Glad we have some time to catch our breath before train time. And yet, it is fun, isn't it—seeing all these people in such a happy holiday mood?"

"Over the river and through the wood, to grandmother's house we go" sang the Pierces to the accompaniment of jingling bells and creaking leather. The runners of their sleigh slipped over the frozen ground, squeaking and crunching their own obbligato. They rushed down the slope, waving as they raced by neighbors returning their greetings and cows munching the hay strewn over banks of snow.

Over in the valley lay Sutter's Mill. Gray smoke spiraled into the frosty air against a background of purple hills and snow-laden pines. Colorfully clad skaters dotted a frozen pond, and the shouts and laughter of the children sifted through the crisp air. Far beyond lay Long Island Sound, where the Atlantic's grey winter waters spattered the shore.

There were eager questions. "How long before we get to New London?" "Do you think we might go to the old Ferry Tavern while we are there?"

Up and down the Connecticut hills the sleigh flew on its way home for Christmas at the old place.

CHRISTMAS
IN THE CITY

"Once upon a time"
Being the sequel to
CHRISTMAS IN THE COUNTRY

That was the year when Uncle Erik and Aunt Stella got the Thorkelsons to care for the farm while they went "up to the city" to spend the Holidays with John and Clara.

Scat!

They took the 6:17 A.M. "accommodation train"

"fresh fruit, chewin' gum, magazines"

Illustrations by LEE MERO

(It "accommodated" freight, livestock and people)

Erik and Stella arrived at the Union Depot, which was even BIGGER than they had imagined!

"A Hack", says Mr Webster, "is a carriage for hire".

An almost endless line of hacks waited to drive folks to their destinations

They got a real thrill, though, when John said they would ride out home in one of the new E-LEC-TRIC CARS -- complete with trailer!

"Faster and more comfortable", he said, as they found seats next to the stove for the two mile ride—

Erik's telescope grip

Yes sir!" said John, "these are going to put horse-cars right out of business!"

Next morning, after the grocer had called for his daily order, everybody left home for a trip downtown, "to go through the stores."

"Just like fairy-land!" exclaimed Stella.

She didn't forget to buy a souvenir coffee spoon for Mrs. Thorkelson

On the way home the Turkey was bought,

Next day, the wood-box was filled to overflowing

Good things fairly popped from the oven!

The Turkey was plucked,

The children had a final rehearsal for the Sunday school program

Uncle Erik "slicked up" his celluloid collar

And a nice goose was sent over to the parsonage

That evening they went over to the Exposition Building to hear the "Messiah"

And Stella got a chance to observe what the ladies up in the city were wearing

On Christmas Eve, the candles were lighted

Clara ALWAYS stood by with a handy pail of water.

As usual, the gifts were "just what everyone wanted!"

Except— Erik's jacket seemed a bit large!

CHRISTMAS MORNING the snow-plows were out early to clear the walks.

The family attended service at one of the BIG churches downtown

(a generous gift from his congregation had made the pastor's dream come true)

"Now, my Son, I can see my way to send you to college"

Cream of Tomato soup
celery olives
pickles
turkey ham
potatoes mashed
peas rutabagas
beet pickles
pineapple sherbet
apple mince
cranberry pie
cheese nuts
coffee milk

Clara planned the customary Christmas dinner. Later, other relatives living in the city dropped in to visit with Erik and Stella and so the turkey got a final going over for the evening lunch

The day after Christmas, being a very nice one for this time of year, John rented a team and a two-seated sleigh and took the family on his favorite ride around the parkways.

Ice-boats made a pretty picture

The Park was thronged with skaters

Stella thought "the Falls" were "just like fairy-land!"

John "saved up" the most exciting entertainment for the last evening! Then, they went to the neighborhood fire-barn, where, promptly at eight, the fire drill took place. The gong rang, the horses pranced to their places, a fireman slid down the pole and "a pleasant time was had by all!"

the Captain

MASCOT OF COMPANY EIGHT

Erik thought "the dappled grays were just wonderful!"

They didn't want to appear too much like "country cousins" while they were with John and Clara, but on the way home, they talked about:

"The man who lit the gas light with a newfangled device on the end of a stick",

"How Clara didn't have to pump water"

And how he thawed it out with a long iron rod when it froze up!"

"Those good, hot chestnuts at five cents a bag"

"The steaming kettle sign for a tea and coffee store"

"All those pieces of Grandma's china that Erik could mend with that new cement the man sold him!"

NEW China CEMENT

"How much they enjoyed the Christmas music"

But, after all, it was good to be "HOME AGAIN" when the Thorkelsons met them at the station with the bob-sled!

(a requested reprint)

In the beginning was the Word, and the Word was with God and the Word was God. He was in the beginning with God; all things were made through him, and without him was not anything made that was made. In him was life, and the life was the light of men. The light shines in the darkness, and the darkness has not overcome it.

And the Word became flesh and dwelt among us, full of grace and truth; we have beheld his glory, glory as of the only Son from the Father.

And from his fulness have we all received, grace upon grace. For the law was given through Moses; grace and truth came through Jesus Christ. ✠ ✠ ✠

John 1:1-5, 14, 16-17

Gloria

The sky was ablaze
with glory
and joy
as angels tumbled their glorias
earthward
which moved like a thousand strings
of harps and lyres
to premiere peace,
now famous in all tongues.
Sheer illumination.
Glory had burst
into sprays and splashes.
Sky and hillside,
heaven and earth,
were enmeshed
in light
and joy
and glory
and God's will.
The earth was ripe
for him.

HERBERT F. BROKERING

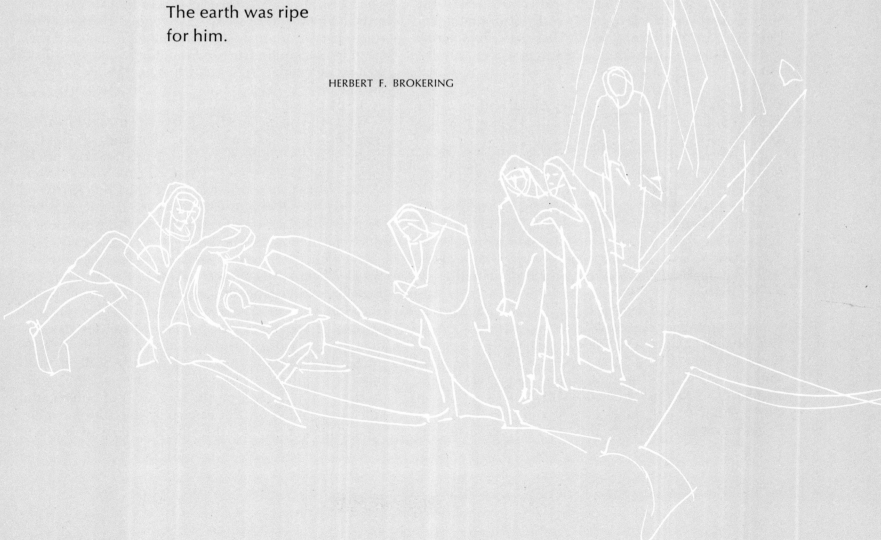

The Gentle Lights of Christmas

DOROTHEA MAGDALENE FOX

Luminarias line the paths and rooflines
of Old Town Plaza in Abuquerque, New Mexico

HAVE you seen the lights of Christmas — the *luminarias*—glowing softly along walks and outlining rooftops where you live? These days, one does not need to travel to New Mexico where the custom originated, to find luminarias. Slowly the custom of using these lights has spread from the Spanish Southwest to the East and the North of our country. Last year, for example, in cold Minnesota, luminarias appeared in several residential districts where families wanted to light their homes and were cutting down on the use of electricity because of the energy crisis. What more lovely light could they have than that of a luminaria, the amber glow of a candle shining through a brown paper bag.

The custom began in the old Southwest—New Mexico and Southwestern Texas—where in early days, the nights of Christmas were illuminated with small bonfires made of fragrant piñon boughs brought down from the mountains to burn on the ground. Later, lights of candles in paper bags burned along driveways, walks, and flat roofs of homes. These were called luminarias. The bonfires, which predated them, were *farolitos*.

In the Southwest, legacies of old Spain and Mexico left an imprint on the people of New Mexico, Texas, and Arizona. One of the ancient customs is the traditional lighting of the little fires and the luminarias. They commemorate the great light that came to the shepherds at the announcement of the coming of the Christ child. Today, shops, homes, and churches make lights to set out on the nights of the Christmas season. A few Spanish families in Santa Fé and Taos, New Mexico, still like to use small bonfires, the farolitos. But it is the luminarias that are the most popular.

The original Spanish custom of the farolitos came with the Conquistadores as they rode north from Old Mexico into the New World. According to early records these fires were seen as long ago as 1626, near the rugged, raw frontier town of Santa Fé that lay sheltered in the Sangre Christo Mountains. The good Fray Alonso Benavides, riding north from Mexico City, reported seeing many fragrant fires of piñon sparkling in the clear evenings.

When the blue-coated military men of the American Occupation forces under the command of General Philip Kearny rode into this same ancient adobe town after 1846, some of the officers wrote letters telling of the strange custom of piles of pinewood fires that blazed at intervals along the narrow winding streets. They gave a cheerful glow to the procession of people going to church on Christmas Eve.

One young observing American officer, Lieutenant W. H. Emory, whose book, *Notes of a Military Reconnaissance*, is a historic memoir, wrote about an interesting visit to the tiny village of Tomé in New Mexico. It was there that he noticed this special custom, not on Christmas Eve, but in the fall of 1846 during the Fiesta Eve celebration. He noticed small piles of wood placed at regular intervals. Some were on the ground, others on the low walls of houses, and still others piled on the turrets of the adobe *copilla*. As darkness crept over the village a signal was given, and the area became alight with flickering fires. Roaring rockets flew from open doors and windows of homes. The church celebrated with rockets too. It was a beautiful sight, joyous and bright with fun, frolic, and light, wrote Lieutenant Emory. These notes on what he experienced became one of the first early American historical writings which described the Old World Spanish custom of farolitos.

With the coming of the first American traders along the old Santa Fé Trail that stretched southwest from Independence, Missouri into New Mexico, came the brown paper bags used by merchants and the people who purchased goods in their stores. After a number of years, the little piñon wood fires were used less and less, until presently they have almost disappeared. It is the luminarias that keep alive the religious custom and shed their luminous lights around the towns and villages during the Christmas season.

Albuquerque, the largest city of New Mexico, has a fine residential area in which luminarias are practically the only outside lights during the Christmas season. In one very large home over 4,000 bags are prepared for the candles which are set along the

Roofs, railings and even chimneys
are decorated with luminarias

HOW TO MAKE A LUMINARIA

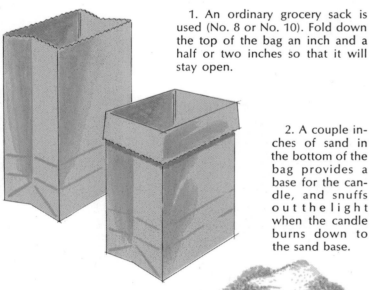

1. An ordinary grocery sack is used (No. 8 or No. 10). Fold down the top of the bag an inch and a half or two inches so that it will stay open.

2. A couple inches of sand in the bottom of the bag provides a base for the candle, and snuffs out the light when the candle burns down to the sand base.

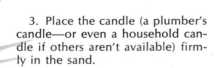

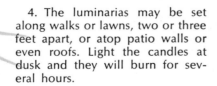

3. Place the candle (a plumber's candle—or even a household candle if others aren't available) firmly in the sand.

4. The luminarias may be set along walks or lawns, two or three feet apart, or atop patio walls or even roofs. Light the candles at dusk and they will burn for several hours.

curbs, walks, driveway, and flat rooftop. Thousands of spectators come from far and near, and those in cars dim the lights so as to get the best effect.

In Albuquerque and Santa Fé, there is a virtual luminaria trail along which people drive and walk to see the beauty of the amber lights against the blackness of the night. This old custom has spread across New Mexico and Texas, north into the Midwest and east to the Middle Atlantic and New England states. In St. Paul, Minnesota, one family lined the broad walk to their church with luminarias as a surprise for those who came to the Christmas Eve services. Seen on a winter night when the snow is falling the radiance is beautiful. These lights create a feeling of reverence that no other traditional decorations can make.

Perhaps one of the most spectacular settings for these lights is in the old Spanish city of El Paso. Even though it is now the largest city on the southern border, the custom has been kept, and on Christmas Eve it is alight with thousands of luminarias. Roofs of houses, lawns, long winding driveways, high walls, and churches are bright with the illumination. Boys and men with long tapers quietly light the candles after sundown and the whole city seems to glow!

Actually, these lights are easily prepared. An ordinary, medium-sized brown paper bag about 12 inches high is used. The top is folded over like a cuff for about two inches to help keep the bag in shape. Sand is placed in the bottom of the bag about three to four inches deep, and a small plumber's candle, or vigil candle, about four inches long, is pressed into the sand. This holds the candle upright and snuffs out the flame when the candle burns low.

Rows of flickering lights on Christmas Eve are a lovely sight. The soft, copperish color adds beauty to the Holy Night.

47

Historic Organs of Europe

DAVID P. DAHL

Historic organs of the past stand as stirring visual and aural reminders of previous cultural traditions. The austere flavor of late medieval Gothic architecture can be seen and heard in some of the few remaining 14th and 15th century organs: The classic concepts of balance, symmetry, and restraint are evident in the 16th century Renaissance organ cases; baroque grandeur and embellishment are apparent in the magnificently ornate organs of the 17th and 18th centuries. For the past 600 years, the Christian church has provided the chief setting for the development of the pipe organ, an instrument which has grown in importance through its liturgical relationship to Christianity.

The organs pictured here are representative of the best in organ building within a historic era; some of them have undergone restoration; all are played regularly for weekly services, recitals, and concerts.

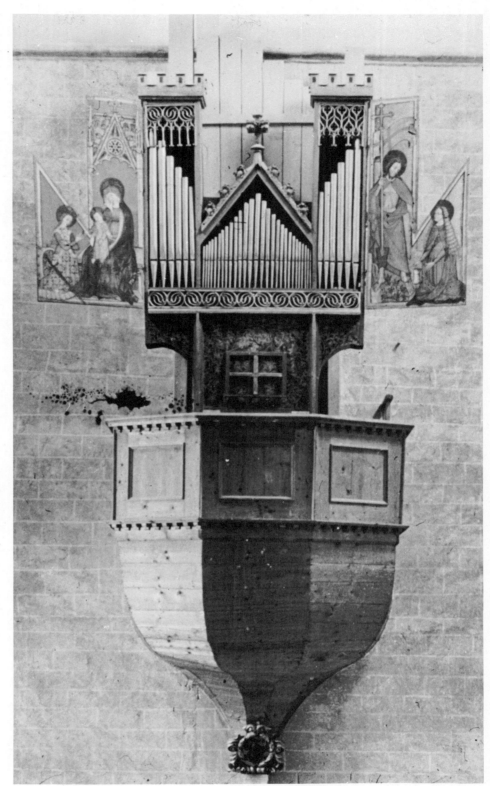

Sion, Switzerland

Some 585 Christmas celebrations have taken place during the life of the organ at the Church of Notre Dame de Valère, Sion, Switzerland. The Gothic organ, built in 1390, is the oldest playable organ in the world. The case of this organ is described as the "swallow nest" type, because it is attached directly to the wall in the west end of the church. Paintings on the winged case doors reflect the other-worldly attitude of Gothic society. Even though some changes were made in the organ in 1718, most of the pipes in this rather small one manual (keyboard) organ remain from the original 14th century installation. The tone of this organ has been described as "strong, glittering, and bell-like," and quite unlike any other organ in the world.

Innsbruck, Austria

Delicacy and a singing, vocal quality typify the essence of early Italian organs. The small, one manual 17th century organ in the *Silbern Kapelle* (Silver Chapel), Innsbruck, Austria, has a facade of wooden pipes rather than the usual metal. Built by an anonymous late Renaissance builder, this organ was a gift from the Roman pontiff. Although not intended for congregational singing, it provided appropriate subtle commentary during the course of liturgical worship.

Helsingør, Denmark

As a young Danish composer, Dietrich Buxtehude held his first job as organist-choirmaster at the *Marienkirche*, Helsingør (Elsinore), Denmark. The organ he played has been recreated in the original casework of 1624. In addition to his skills as organist and composer, Buxtehude is remembered for the *Abendmusiken* (evening concerts) which he later developed in Lübeck for the Sundays in Advent.

Paris, France

The brilliantly innovative organ builder, Aristide Cavaillé-Coll, established a totally new tradition in the romantic 19th century. Among the largest of his 'symphonic' concert organs is the five manual organ with 100 draw-stops (each controlling separate sets of pipes), built in 1862 and located in the Church of St. Sulpice. This organ was not created for congregational singing, since there was none, nor for work with choral groups. A second ('choir') organ located in the front of the church is used with choirs. The larger organ is located in the rear gallery and is used as a solo instrument. This organ can still be heard during weekly Sunday services, especially in the grand improvisation with which the organist traditionally concludes the mass. Among the great organists to preside over this organ was Marcel Dupré (1886-1971). Organist at St. Sulpice for over 30 years, his "Variations on a Noël," a set of colorful variations on an old French Christmas carol, is one of his best known compositions for organ.

Lübeck, Germany

A relatively small old organ of exceptional beauty stands in the Church of St. Jakobi in Lübeck, Germany. This organ, originally built around 1500, has been one of the significant instruments responsible for the revival of interest in the "classic" principles of organ building. The main organ case has an essentially Renaissance flavor, with its straight lines, flat front, and balanced symmetry. Only the tops of the two towers, with their carved traceries covering the ends of the pipes, betray a lingering Gothic element. Early in the 17th century a *Rückpositiv* was added. This is a smaller organ case containing pipes played from the lowest keyboard. It is located in the foreground, and is suspended from the gallery rail. There is more ornateness in its curving facade than there is in the rest of the organ, showing the change in architectural emphasis which emerged in the baroque period. Among the famous organist-composers associated with this organ is Hugo Distler (1908-1942) whose variations on the Advent hymn, "Savior of the Nations, Come," blend ancient styles and material with modern in a fresh, original manner.

Haarlem, Holland

Surely one of the most famous organs in the world is the one built by Christian Müller for the Church of St. Bavo in Haarlem, Holland, in 1735. It is the ultimate in grandeur and magnificence of the baroque aesthetic. The total height of the organ case is about 60 feet. Over a dozen carved figures, many playing musical instruments, decorate the elaborate, hand carved, gilded case. To have such an immodest organ seems a contradiction to the basic teachings of the Dutch Reformed Church, whose Calvinistic beliefs encouraged simplicity and austerity. The explanation is that the organ was commissioned and is still owned by the city and not the church. It was considered a symbol of the honor, prestige, and wealth of the community. Immaculately restored, this organ produces one of the most splendid sounds imaginable, and is further enhanced by superbly reverberant acoustics. Among the famous musicians to perform on this large instrument are Handel, Mozart, and Liszt.

Amsterdam, Holland

The beloved Christmas choral motet, "Hodie Christus Natus Est," was written by Jan Pieterszoon Sweelinck of the Netherlands in the late 16th century. Sweelinck, who was one of Holland's most famous composers, was equally well known as an organist and teacher. The smaller of the two organs which he played at the *Oude Kerk* (Old Church) in Amsterdam has been recreated in its original form as the two manual and pedal instrument was first built by Niehoff and Jansz, 1544-1545. The winged case doors give a protective cover and provide a striking element of design, but they also help to project the sound of the organ into the church.

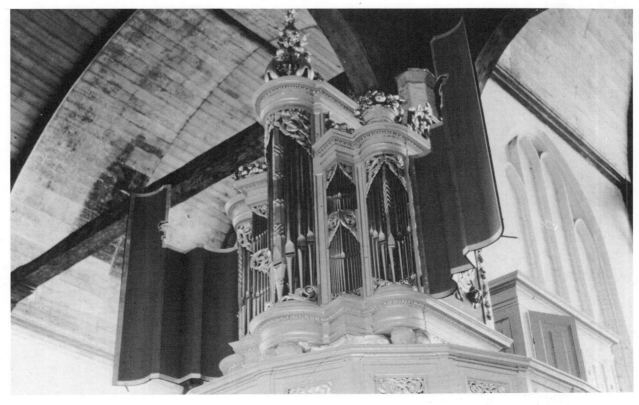

Lüneburg, Germany

When he was a choir boy at the nearby *Michaeliskirche*, J. S. Bach spent at least one Christmas in this north German village. And undoubtedly, when he was in his teens, he often played this organ at the *Johanniskirche*. Originally built in 1551 by Hendrik Niehoff, the organ was considerably enlarged in the baroque 17th century. The pedal was increased, and the *Rückpositiv*, which is visible in the foreground, was added. Rich embellishment, including carved angels playing musical instruments, typify the polychrome case. The organ delivers a brilliant and scintillating sound, well suited to the music of Bach.

Gimont, France

This rather small town in southern France is the home of a remarkable example of 18th century French classic organ building. Fortunately, the town has been too poor to improve the organ, so it remains one of the very few instruments left untampered from this era. In the 18th century the popular French Christmas carols, called *Noels* inspired a number of composers, including Louis Couperin, Louis Claude D'Aquin, Nicholas Lebegue, and Claude Balbastre, to compose considerable sets of variations on these tunes. These pieces require the bold, nasal, and exotic sounding stops which are typical of French classic organs—stops like the *trompette, cromorne, cornet,* and *voix humaine.* The original pedal board of this organ still exists as it did when the organ was built in 1722 by the German builder, Godefroy Schmitt. Instead of the more conventional pedal keys, there are elongated buttons which control the pipes of the pedal division.

Neuenfelde, Germany

One of the most important organ builders of all time was the great Arp Schnitger, who died in 1719, and whose home was the small village of Neuenfelde, near Hamburg, Germany. He completed this instrument for his own parish church in 1688. This two manual organ contains a rich palette of colors and sonorities appropriate to the liturgical tradition of the Lutheran heritage, especially the organ chorale. The inscription painted on the ceiling over the organ perfectly sums up the *raison d'etre* for an organ: *"Alles was Odem hat, Lobe den Herren"*—"All that has breath, praise the Lord."

Isaac Watts, Hymnodist

AUSTIN C. LOVELACE

HAVE you ever sat in church, bored with the hymns? A young man of 15 named Isaac Watts (1674-1748) did and told his father so, to which his father replied, "If you don't like the psalms we sing why don't you write something better?" Watts, who was a semi-invalid most of his life, had a fertile, powerful mind and was disturbed by the condition of psalm singing in church. He wrote "To see the dull indifference, the negligent and thoughtless air, that sits upon the faces of the whole assembly while the psalm is on their lips, might tempt even a charitable observer to suspect the fervour of inward religion; and it is much to be feared that the minds of most of the worshippers are absent or unconcerned."

Up to the time of Watts, hymn singing was more or less illegal in church, and only versions of the psalms were sung. In some places the "Old Version" by Sternhold and Hopkins still could be heard, but most sang the "New Version" by Tate and Brady. But these often tried to keep to the exact meaning of the original Hebrew, creating awkward lines and atrocious rhymes. Watts's aim was to see "David converted into a Christian" and to modernize the psalms so that they had meaning for people in worship. In 1719 he published *The Psalms of David imitated in the language of the New Testament, and apply'd to the Christian state of worship*—no small undertaking! Such hymns as "Before Jehovah's aweful throne," "Jesus shall reign," and "O God, our help in ages past" are all based on the psalms.

His second contribution was perhaps even more important—hymns of human composure. He asked, if Christ makes all things new, why must our praises remain in the Old Covenant? So he turned to writing new hymns, sometimes based on New Testament thought but often on original ideas. Because he wrote them so well he opened the door to other poets, and the flood of modern hymnody began. His collections were *Horae Lyrica* (1705), *Hymns and Spiritual Songs* (1707), *Divine Songs for Children* (1715), and *The Psalms of David Imitated* (1719).

His success can be laid to his abilities as a fine poet, as well as his ability to write hymns which the common man could sing and understand. He used few large words, most being of only one syllable, and his fidelity to Scripture, his objective (rather than subjective) treatment of material, his clearness of language, and the lyrical quality of his verse made people want to sing. He used only a few basic meters (mostly common, short, and long), which made it easy to sing his hymns to familiar tunes.

Mention has been made of Watts's *Divine Songs for Children,* and hymnody is indebted to him for opening a door to this area which had never been considered before. He wrote 28 hymns for children, mostly with a theme of praise. The most famous is "I sing th' almighty power of God," filled with marvelous imagery.

While many of his hymns have disappeared from use today because of their heavy Calvinist doctrine, his finest still stand as an example of how to write a great hymn. His hymns always stick to a single theme and have organic unity, a bold and memorable first line, and a progression of thought leading to an incisive climax (Watts wrote a textbook on logic which was used in English universities for 100 years). As Millar Patrick has written, "His hymns are brief, compact, direct, and telling." When James Montgomery says that Watts was "the real founder of English hymnody," he is recognizing that it was Watts who broke the stranglehold of psalmody, made hymn singing popular and respectable, and persuaded the church that singing the gospel was just as important as preaching it.

Joy to the World

Some hymns are popular in spite of the words! The magnificent opening line and first, second, and last stanzas are the epitome of this great hymn. The third stanza is outdated theology and is often omitted when the hymn is sung.

The text is based on the second half of Psalm 98, with echoes of Genesis 3:17-18 and Romans 5:20. Watts has turned it into a Christian song of rejoicing—a Christmas carol instead of a Jewish psalm. The psalmist of course does not talk of Christ, and actually neither does Watts, directly. But the theme is of the Lord and Savior who has come to the world.

The tune "Antioch" was arranged by the American musician Lowell Mason around 1836, and was first published in the *Modern Psalmist* (Boston, 1839) with the notation "from Handel." At best it can be said the tune is based on fragments from Handel's *Messiah*. The opening phrase is similar to the opening of "Lift up your heads," or perhaps more likely the tenor part of "Glory to God" (the tune is in the tenor, really!). The fuguing section with echoing parts has some similarity to the introduction to "Comfort ye." While the result may be patchwork, it makes a very attractive quilt of music and is most comfortable and enjoyable to sing.

53

Joy to the World

Isaac Watts

Melody arr., Lowell Mason

1. Joy to the world, the Lord is come! Let earth re-
2. Joy to the world, the Sav-ior reigns! Let men their
3. No more let sins and sor-rows grow, Nor thorns in-
4. He rules the world with truth and grace, And makes the

ceive her King; Let ev-ery heart pre-pare him
songs em-ploy, While fields and floods, rocks, hills and
fest the ground; He comes to make his bless-ings
na-tions prove The glo-ries of his right-eous-

room, And heaven and na-ture sing, And heaven and na-ture
plains Re-peat the sound-ing joy, Re-peat the sound-ing
flow Far as the curse is found, Far as the curse is
ness, And won-ders of his love, And won-ders of his

And heaven and na-ture sing, and

sing, And heaven and heaven and na-ture sing.
joy, Re-peat, re-peat the sound-ing joy.
found, Far as, far as the curse is found.
love, And won-ders, won-ders of his love.

heaven and na-ture sing,

Mary

Herbert Brokering

Robert Wetzler

1. Mar-y took the swad-dling cloth to bind it on the child
2. Mar-y took the sweet per-fume to pour it on the man
3. Mar-y took the spice and myrrh to lay it on the Lord

Je - sus, and Je - sus was pre - pared _____ to
Je - sus, and Je - sus was pre - pared _____ to
Je - sus, and Je - sus was pre - pared _____ to

live, to live on the earth.
die, to die for the earth.
rise, to rise from the earth.

Bethlehem Star

Herbert Brokering

Tune, David N. Johnson

1. Beth - le - hem star lead all the gaz - ing;
2. Cat - tle and sheep, new-born cre - a - tion;
3. An - gels on high, tell out the mean - ing; sing to the Lord ____
4. Peo - ple a - stir, sleep in the pil - lows;
5. Peace in dis - guise, break out in glo - ry;

____ a new song.

Wise Men from far, faith so a - maz - ing;
All things that weep in - side the na - tion,
Shep-herds ask why; kneel and come lean - ing;
Ros - es and fir, cold weep-ing wil - lows;
All who are wise, be in the sto - ry;

sing to the Lord ____ a new song.

Refrain

He has done mar -

Tune from **Twelve Folksongs and Spirituals,** copyright © 1968 Augsburg Publishing House. Harmonization by Jan Bender, from Contemporary Worship 1: **Hymns,** copyright 1969, by permission of publishers for Inter-Lutheran Commission on Worship.

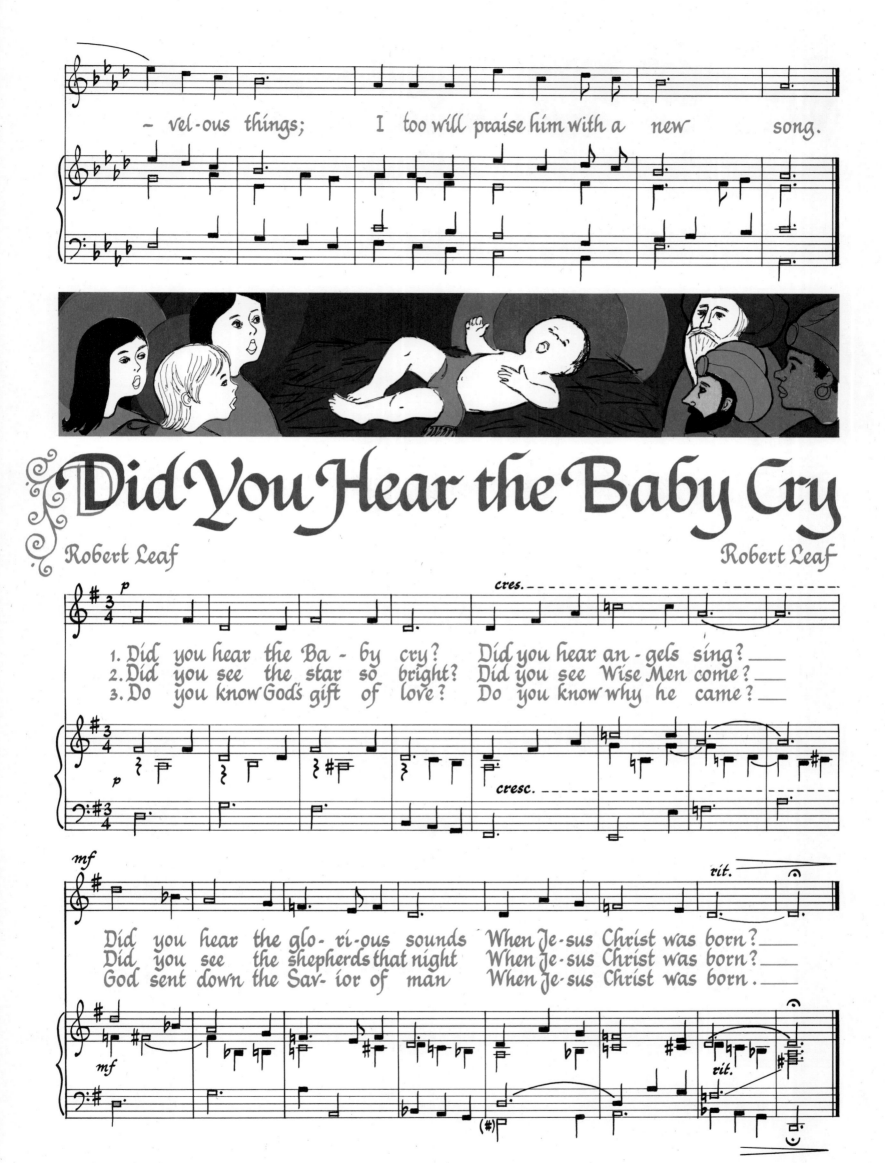

- vel-ous things; I too will praise him with a new song.

Did You Hear the Baby Cry

Robert Leaf   Robert Leaf

cres.

1. Did you hear the Ba - by cry? Did you hear an - gels sing?____
2. Did you see the star so bright? Did you see Wise Men come?____
3. Do you know God's gift of love? Do you know why he came?____

cresc.

Did you hear the glo - ri - ous sounds When Je-sus Christ was born?____
Did you see the shepherds that night When Je-sus Christ was born?____
God sent down the Sav - ior of man When Je-sus Christ was born.____

mf *rit.*

Who Is He in Yonder Stall?

I-to Loh *

English version : Marion A. Lien

I-to Loh

What Khòa"
看

Child lies se-rene-ly in yon stall? Can king-ly crown rest on one so
Eng- jî tî bé-chô lāi, Bók-chiá lâi kūi lóh kèng
聖 嬰 安 臥 槽 中, 牧 人 來 拜 瞻 聖

small? Sing! sing, my soul, your
pài. Sī goá Chú!
客. 是 我 主!

Christmas Carol

Edith Osborne Ives

Edith Osborne Ives
Arr., Charles E. Ives

First Great American Composer

CHARLES E. IVES (1874-1954)

JOHANNES RIEDEL

NINETEEN hundred seventy-four marks the 100th anniversary of the birth of Charles E. Ives, first great American composer. As a composer, Ives incorporated into his compositions the *Gebrauchsmusik* of his daily surroundings. His environment was national and religious. He drew on American barn dances, patriotic songs, popular tunes, marches, gospel songs, and ragtime. His aesthetic was to create out of many disparate elements a music which reflected the life he saw around him.

Thus when turn-of-the-century American composers were producing Europe-oriented music, Ives was the independent anticipator of 20th century techniques. Some of his music, written between 1888 and 1928, includes blatant polytonality, massive tone clusters, complex rhythms and meters, advanced dissonances, microtones, and tone rows. His music anticipated by many years the compositional techniques of the most advanced contemporary music—devices that came to be associated with Béla Bartók, Igor Stravinsky, Paul Hindemith, and Arnold Schönberg. Thus Ives stands at the musical gateway to the 20th century. His example still lends strength to composers who hope to speak for themselves and for their times.

The most important aspect of Ives' music, however, is not his development of previously unexplored areas of compositional techniques, but rather his use of all musical materials in a very general sense. Ives' music includes all possible kinds of musical materials, organized into compositions. He did not acknowledge an artistic hierarchy in the various kinds of music.

Popular music of his time, which was as much a part of his life as any other style, was brought together with music of a totally different nature. In bringing together art music and the popular music of his local surroundings, he created in his compositions a musical reality which was more comprehensive than that of any previous composer.

Ives also brought together contrasting styles and techniques of composition. Within a given piece one may find side by side 19th and 20th century devices, banalities and breathtaking experiments, traditional forms and futuristic organizational principles, trite harmony and chords amalgamating all twelve tones of the octave.

Charles Ives' compositions were undoubtedly influenced by the musical interests of his father, George, who received a thorough musical education in New York. At the age of 17 he organized

his musical acquaintances to form the Connecticut Volunteer Band. He was active in the musical life of Danbury, Conn., leading bands and choirs as well as giving music lessons. George Ives was a man who would indulge in experimentations with musical instruments. He would attempt to recreate at the piano the sound of the off-pitch church bell. Stretching many violin strings, he would tune them in multiple ways. As a late successor of Benjamin Franklin, he would experiment with glasses and bells. Experimenting with echoes, he would play his instruments one at a time over the city pond, which enlarged the echo that returned to him. He divided his band, locating individual instruments at several distances and at different heights. His son divided the orchestra in this fashion in such works as *The Unanswered Question* and Symphony no. 4.[1]

The Ives family goes back to the early days of America when, in 1635, William Ives sailed from Dorchester, England, to Boston. Isaac Ives, great-grandfather of Charles, moved the family to Danbury and purchased the house which was to be the Ives family home for the next four generations.

The generations of the Ives' family consisted of people who were prominent in the life of the community. As bankers and businessmen, they belonged to the upper echelon of Danburian society and took an active interest in the economic, cultural, and spiritual progress of Danbury.

Influenced by the rich heritage of the Ives family, Charles was not only a composer, but also a writer. His writings were concerned with matters which were of vital importance to him: music, life insurance business, and politics. His essays include titles such as *Essays Before a Sonata*, "Postface" to *114 Songs*, "The Amount to Carry — Measuring the Prospect: Formulas Which Will Guide and Assist the Agent in Making Proper Adjustment of Insurance Protection To Carrying Ability and Needs," "The Majority," "Concerning a Twentieth Amendment." His writings on music sometimes amounted to marginal notes for his scores. Thus the beginning of *Psalm 90* shows the remark "God's eternity" at the opening chord. The second chord reads "Creation," the third chord "God's wrath against sin (flood, etc.)," the fourth mentions "Prayer and humility." Many of his writings show a close affinity with God. Thus an important theme in his *Essays Before a Sonata* is the apprehension of spiritual values. He was influenced in these views by the writings of the transcenden-

Music is one of the many ways God has of beating in on man —
his life, his ideals, his hope in everything—
an inner something, a spiritual storm, a something else that stirs the man in one of his parts (consciousness) and "all at once"—
we roughly call these parts (as a kind of entity) "soul"—

it acts thro or vibrates, or couples up to human sensations in ways (or measures) man may hear and know: that is, he knows he hears them and says (or thinks or feels) he knows them.—

further than this, what this inner something is which begets all this, is something no one knows — especially those who define it and use it primarily to make a living.—

all this means almost nothing to those who will think about it — music — that no one knows what it is — and the less he knows he knows what it is the nearer it is to music — probably.[2]

Majority
The Masses! The Masses!
The Masses have toiled,
Behold the works of the
World!
The Masses are thinking,
Whence comes the thought
of the World!

The Masses are singing,
are singing, singing,
Whence comes the
Art of the World!
The Masses are yearning,
are yearning, are yearning,
Whence comes the hope
of the World.
The Masses are dreaming,
dreaming,
The Masses are dreaming,
Whence come the visions
of God!
God's in His Heaven,
All will be well
with the World! [5]

Everything from a mule to an
oak which nature has given
life has a right to that life,
and a right to throw into that
life all the values it can.
Whether they be approved
by a human mind or seen
with a human eye is no
concern of that right. The
right of a tree, wherever
it stands, is to grow as strong
and as beautiful as it can
whether seen or unseen,
whether made immortal by a
Turner, or translated into a
part of Seraphic architecture
or a kitchen table. The
instinctive and progressive
interest of every man in
art, we are willing to affirm
with no qualification, will go
on and on, ever fulfilling
hopes, ever building new
ones, ever opening new
horizons, until the day will
come when every man while
digging his potatoes will
breathe his own epics, his
own symphonies (operas,
he likes it); and as he sits of
an evening in his backyard
and shirt sleeves smoking his
pipe and watching his brave
children in their fun of
building their themes for
their sonatas of their life, he
will look up over the
mountains and see his visions
in their reality, will hear the
transcendental strains of the
day's symphony responding
in their many choirs, and in
all their perfection, through
the west wind and the tree
tops! [5](pp. 128-129)

62

talists of Concord, Massachusetts: Emerson, Hawthorne, the Alcotts, and Thoreau. Their transcendental philosophy became the basis of Ives' philosophy on life, which he expanded and applied to music in an attempt to explain and justify his art in relationship—to the art of others, to nature, to the universe, to God, to morals, to truth, to Americanism, and to mysticism.

Ives lived two full lives, that of a life insurance executive and that of a composer. For about 30 years he sold insurance during the day and composed music at night, on weekends and vacations. In a relatively short time, Ives progressed from clerk to an insurance partnership with Julian Myrick in 1907.

Their partnership became one of the most successful of the time. The *New York Times* called their business phenomenal. Between 1908 and 1930 they sold a half billion dollars worth of insurance.[2] Much of their success is credited to Ives' innovative techniques. He established a training school for agents which has been much imitated. He also developed a concept of estate planning, now a basic principle.

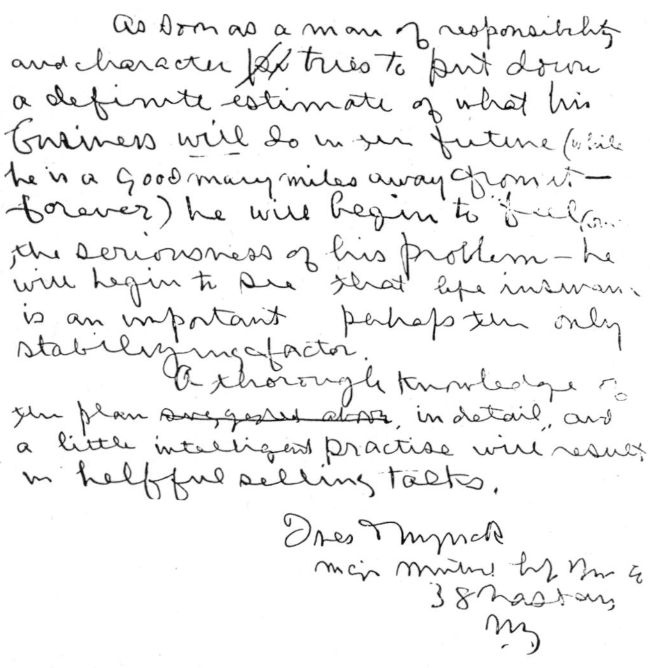

[handwritten letter]

As soon as a man of responsibility and character tries to put down a definite estimate of what his business will do in the future (while he is a good many miles away from it — forever) he will begin to feel the seriousness of his problem — he will begin to see that life insurance is an important perhaps the only stabilizing factor. A thorough knowledge of the plan in detail, and a little intelligent practise will result in helpful selling facts.

Ives & Myrick
main...
38 Nassau
N.Y.

Recognizing the great merits of Ives' contributions, the College of Life Insurance, New York, granted Ives a posthumous humanities award in 1965, 11 years after his death.

The years in which Ives was launching his life insurance career were simultaneously his most productive years as a composer (1905-1916). The large body of his music includes four symphonies, six sonatas (two for piano and four for violin), two string quartets, and a host of smaller works for ensembles of various and often uncommon instruments. Also included among the orchestral works are *The Unanswered Question, Central Park*

in the Dark, Three Places in New England, and *Holidays*.

Ives also wrote a number of choral works, both sacred and secular, and several works for organ. His most complete body of work is the enormous number of songs (around 200), which he wrote over the 30 years from 1888-1928. His first compositions as well as his last were songs.

As a young person in Danbury, Charles Ives experienced the impressive camp meetings of the Methodists at nearby Redding. He comments in his *Memos* about these outdoor services:

I remember, when I was a boy — at the outdoor Camp Meeting services in Redding, all the farmers, their families and field hands, for miles around, would come afoot or in their farm wagons. I remember how the great waves of sound used to come through the trees — when things like *Beulah Land, Woodworth, Nearer, my God, to thee, The Shining Shore, Nettleton, In the Sweet Bye and Bye* and the like were sung by thousands of "let out" souls. The music notes and words on paper were about as much like what they "were" (at those moments) as the monogram on a man's necktie may be like his face. Father, who led the singing, sometimes with his cornet or his voice, sometimes with both voice and arms, and sometimes in the quieter hymns with a French horn or violin, would always encourage the people to sing their own way. Most of them knew the words and music (theirs) by heart, and sang it that way. If they threw the poet or composer around a bit, so much the better for the poetry and the music. There was power and exaltation in these great conclaves of sound from humanity.[3]

At the age of 13, Charles assumed an organist position at the West Street Congregational Church in his hometown. The next year he became organist at the First Baptist Church. A typical organ program of Ives at his church would be like his presentation of church music on Easter Sunday, April 6, 1889 (evening service):

Prelude:	*Andante comodo*, Scharwenka
Anthem:	*Why seek ye the Living among the Dead?*, G. B. Nevin
Offertory:	*The Lord of Life Is Risen Again* (male quartet), T. C. Fairbanks
Postlude:	*Allegro maestoso* in G Minor, D. Buck
	Three-part Invention no. 1, J. S. Bach

Less than two years later he was praised in a local newspaper for his "patient perseverance in his study of the organ" and was congratulated on his "marked ability as a master of the keys."

Ives continued his church music career by serving as organist at the Centre Church on the Green while at Yale University (1894-1899). He later assumed the post of organist-choirmaster at the First Presbyterian Church, Bloomfield, New Jersey (1899-1900), and at the Central Presbyterian Church in New York City (1900-1902).

The Ives homestead in Danbury, Connecticut

Charles E. Ives

During his fifteen years as an organist, Ives was exposed to several liturgical traditions: Methodist, Baptist, Congregational, and Presbyterian. He was therefore steeped in church music idioms which ranged from rural revivalism to metropolitan church worship services. The majority of his work was done from the background of the Reformed and Free Church tradition of the Congregational and Presbyterian denominations.

Many of his early choral works were left behind at the churches he served and were eventually lost or thrown out. Ives wrote a number of choral psalms which, in the Reformed tradition, had their place as a regular morning anthem. One of his psalms *(Psalm 135)* was designated to be sung as an anthem-processional. A cantata and three harvest chorales are also among his choral writings.

Among the several organ variations on hymn tunes and other organ pieces for church written by Ives are:

Variations on *Jerusalem the Golden*	1888-1897
Variations on *America*	1891-1892?
Interludes for hymns	1892-1895?

1. Interlude for *Nettleton (Come, Thou Fount of every blessing)*
2. Interlude for *Bethany (Nearer, my God, to thee)*
3. Interlude for *Eventide (Abide with me)*
4. Interlude for *Woodworth (Just as I am)*

Adeste fideles in an organ prelude	1897[4]

Early organ compositions came eventually to exercise a prominent role in his orchestral and chamber works. The first movement of Symphony no. 1 was adapted from an organ sonata played in part at Centre Church; the third movement was adapted from an organ prelude played at the same church. The third movement of *Three Places in New England* also suggests the adaptation of organ pedal lines. Ives also composed a large number of art songs which deal with religious or quasi-religious texts by transcendentalists, gospel hymn writers, and Ives himself.

Some, like *Abide With Me,* use well known hymn tunes. *At the River* is a dissonant setting of the Moody-Sankey hymn. *The Last Reader* uses two hymn tunes (*Cherith* by Spohr and *Manoah* by Haydn).

The inclusion of musical quotations from hymns and spirituals continued throughout Ives' career. The use of these common tunes in his symphonies, sonatas, and art songs reveal his desire to be understood. In his Epilogue of the *Essays Before a Sonata* he noted:

> The man "born down to Babbitt's Corners" may find a deep appeal in the simple but acute Gospel hymns... which ... carries him nearer the "Christ of the people" than does the *Te Deum* of the greatest cathedral.[5]

In setting religious thought to music, Ives' desire to be understood is seen in still another facet. As a young organist he had to come to terms with those in the congregation who objected to his dissonances. He finally decided that he was not justified in interfering with his listeners' spiritual states of mind.

> In playing [new music] at a service: — Is one justified in doing something which to him is quite in keeping with his understanding and feelings? How about the congregation ... who might naturally misunderstand and be disturbed ... a public audience, or a congregation, has some rights.[6]

Ives wrote a number of pieces which are associated with the celebration of Christmas in one way or another. About 1897 he wrote a small choral piece entitled *A Christmas Carol.* In December 1901, a processional was composed, based on the Christmas-associated text *Let There Be Light.* The work was scored for male chorus (or trombones), strings, and organ, and was dedicated to the choir of the Central Presbyterian Church, New York City. Ives wrote, in 1897, an organ prelude based on the Christmas-associated tune, *Adeste fideles.*

Ives' use of Lowell Mason's tune in the First Sonata for violin and piano

In December 1924, Edith Osborne Ives, Ives' daughter, wrote an original poem and tune entitled *Christmas Carol*. The following November, Charles Ives furnished an accompaniment and placed it among his solo songs. The Advent tune and text, *Watchman, tell us of the night,* was used by Ives in 1913 as the basis of a song for soprano with piano accompaniment.

At Christmastime in 1887, Ives wrote a march for brass band entitled *Holiday March* (or as noted on some of the instrumental parts, *Holiday Quickstep*). This piece was played by the Wooster Band of Danbury and is said to have been performed on Christmas Day, 1888, at the Methodist Sunday school. It survives only in a set of parts, written in the hand of Ives' father, for piccolo, two cornets in A, two violins, and piano. Another piece written for brass band and based on a Christmas-associated tune was the *Slow March*, which uses *Adeste fideles* as a *cantus firmus*. However, the piece was intended for the Decoration Day ceremonies in Danbury and was played by the Danbury band on that day in the year 1886 or 1887. No trace of this piece survives.

When Ives quotes particular hymn tunes or popular tunes within a composition, he makes use of a variety of methods. Sometimes the tune appears as a literal citation, often as only a fragment. In other instances the tune is slightly varied without losing its character.

Another method used by Ives is to integrate the tune into the composition. Thus, literally quoted material appears in fragments which are sprinkled liberally throughout. Sometimes in the construction of the melody Ives uses a particular motive to develop a hymnlike melody which is only superficially related to its source.

The works of Ives reveal a number of quotations of Christmas-associated texts and tunes. The citation of Lowell Mason's tune, *Watchman, tell us of the night,* is similarly executed in the First Sonata for violin and piano (1903-1908), Symphony no. 4 (1910-1916), and the song setting, *Watchman* (1913). In each case the melody is quoted in its entirety.

The theme and general makeup of the first movement of Symphony no. 4 had been a part of the First Sonata for violin and piano. Ives noted the content of the movement as consisting of "the searching questions of 'What?' and 'Why?,' which the spirit of man asks of life. . . . The three succeeding movements are the diverse answers in which existence replies." The choir sings the Ad-

vent text of *Watchman* in a manner that is just audible, as if from a distance. The tune itself is surrounded by other citations, namely, fragments of *Nearer, my God, to thee, I hear thy welcome voice,* and Sullivan's *Proprior Deo,* while the celeste intones the Westminster bells.

In the third movement of the First Sonata for violin and piano, Ives uses the tune of *Watchman* in a two-fold way: first, the material of the tune itself; and second, the motive which will, in the piano, clangorously accompany the final hymn citation.

After 1916, Ives' work began to receive public attention. Among the early concerts were Lenore Purcell's 1920 performance of the *Concord* Sonata and John Kirkpatrick's performance of the same work at Town Hall in 1939. The first recording of an Ives work was made in 1934, and in 1937 Lehman Engel led his Madrigal Singers in a recording of *Psalm 67*. In the 1930s most of Ives' support came from fellow composers who not only understood the problems of having new ideas accepted, but also appreciated the complexities, strength, and inspiration of his writing. These younger musicians included Henry Bellamann, Henry Cowell, John Becker, Nicolas Slonimsky, Lou Harrison, Carl Ruggles, and John Kirkpatrick.

In the 1940s this appreciation grew among many musicians and among an enlarged listening audience as well. In 1948, Robert Shaw and the Collegiate Chorale performed *Psalm 67* and the *Harvest Home* Chorales in Carnegie Hall. Ives gained world recognition with the winning of a Pulitzer Prize in 1947, and in 1951 the premiere of his Symphony no. 2 was conducted by Leonard Bernstein.

Acceptance and recognition of Ives' music is increasing today, as is indicated by more performances of his works, television programs featuring his music, new recordings of his works, and courses on Ives being offered in colleges and universities throughout the country.

[1] Peter Yates, *Twentieth Century Music* (New York: Pantheon Books, division of Random House, 1967), p. 256-257.
[2] Eric Salzman, "Insurance" in *New York Times* (June 25, 1961).
[3] John Kirkpatrick, ed., *Charles E. Ives Memos* (New York: W. W. Norton and Company, 1972), p. 132.
[4] Jeffrey Wasson for the Minnesota Centennial Ives Festival, on April 21, 1974, in Minneapolis, Minn.
[5] Howard Boatwright, ed., *Essays Before a Sonata, The Majority and Other Writings by Charles Ives* (New York: W. W. Norton and Company, 1970), p. 124.
[6] Henry and Sidney Cowell, *Charles Ives and His Music* (New York: Oxford University Press, 1955), p. 43-44.
[7] John Kirkpatrick, ed., *A Temporary Mimeographed Catalogue of the Music Manuscripts of Charles Edward Ives (1874-1954) given by Mrs. Ives to the Library of the Yale School of Music, September, 1955* (Library of the Yale School of Music, Copyright 1960 by John Kirkpatrick), p. III.
[8] Charles E. Ives, *114 Songs* (Redding, Conn.: C. E. Ives, 1922), p. 1ff.

The Art of Feeding Winter Birds

BILL BURNSON

Enter now, with little fanfare, a new season into full white flower. It's one of our longest and most gratifying—the *winter bird feeding season*. Season "hunting" dates, fall to spring, are set by nature—not by law. License fees are an amalgam of concern and warm hearts. There's no age limit. The hours are dawn to dusk. For those who have neither strength nor inclination to tramp the winter woods, bird watching from easy "inside" chairs is the ideal winter sport.

Finally, no "limits" apply except for the accusing consciences of those base and faithless sluggards who, forgetful of extreme avian need in these wintry times, fail to keep their feeders full.

Those winter birds need us now! The summer idyll, the long, balmy days with food and comfort aplenty for summer feathered residents is long gone. Now it is time to understand the wants of our winter friends.

Despite the desperate perils in their daily lives, the mixed "bag" (loosely defined as "snowbirds") are a chirpy and vigorous lot. Varieties change from locality to locality and usually include sprightly chickadees, nuthatches, grosbeaks, and the downy and hairy woodpeckers—which were on the summer scene as well.

Nature, with incomparable artistry, has contrived fantastic aid to help birds through cold winters. Avian hearts beat scores of times per minute. And bird temperatures often run above 110 degrees to keep heat in those tiny frames. New feathers grow, and attached muscles fluff them out so that their soft down expands into near perfect air-absorption insulation. Even so, it strains comprehension that fragile winter birds like chickadees and nuthatches can pack in sufficient fuel to survive bitter nights.

Friends of birds can learn from the custom and experiences of polar explorers and natives of the far north (who augment their diet with vastly increased amounts of fat and proteins) of the fuels which neutralize cold.

In these days of arctic chill and deep snow, the snowbirds' essential needs telescope onto one word—*food*. That food is best when it's high in energy sources.

Thoughtful feeders provide these needs with a basic diet of sunflower and mixed bird seed, suet and kitchen fats. But the friends the birds love most are those, and their name is legion, who go a bit further. They add delicacies and variety to the mundane mix. These foods, ranging from the economical to real ambrosia types, include cracked wheat or corn, chicken scratch feed, bread crumbs, chopped nuts and peanut butter, apples, raisins—even grain screenings.

A good neighbor (bird feeders are extra good neighbors) is a skilled advocate of the popular high fat and protein cafeteria feeding—so loved by birds in cold weather. She saves and refrigerates kitchen fats and appropriate leftovers during the summer. Later she melts this mixture and adds oatmeal, bird seeds, and big chunks of suet. This combination is packed into milk cartons with quarter-inch dowels for perches punctured into the sides. When frozen, the cartons are stripped away. This "mass" is hung or placed with a screen of chicken wire as a conserving measure against marauders.

You can make a bird pudding by using these ingredients: 5½ cups oatmeal, 3½ cups corn meal or grits, 3½ cups farina, 1 pound lard, and 12 ounces peanut butter. The procedure: boil 2 cups of the oatmeal in 4 cups of water, stir in the balance. Form this thick mixture into balls or other desired shapes. Refrigerate as needed. And don't hesitate to improvise—as mood and available ingredients allow.

65

Many bird-enamored humans favor the peanut butter log. They use a two-foot length of birch, four to eight inches thick. Into this they bore holes an inch to two in diameter into which are driven small pegs for feeding perches. The holes are filled with peanut butter or other bird goodies, and the log is hung from a convenient tree branch. These logs are practical, eye appealing—and photogenic!

Our "neighbor who knows all" (bird feeders are always extra smart) says, "We throw in every leftover but the kitchen sink. The birds love it and us, too!"

And if your dog shudders and whines in his sleep, it is probably from subliminal anxiety-resentment neuroses caused by the mortifying fact that ground dog biscuits and canned dog food are also practical peerless bird foods.

Feeds and equipment are a solid adjunct to winter business. Many super markets and hardware stores stock bird essentials. While handy men and do-it-yourselfers head for local libraries for practical ideas on building bird shelters and feeders, the affluent will fill these needs from the wide range of feeders, simple to deluxe, available at these stores.

Many times merchants are bird feeders and innovators. One such in our area features low priced balls of ground suet, impregnated with birdseed. Attached to a cord, with a center bar anchor, these balls are a ready-made (and also easily duplicated) aerial lunch counter when swung from branch or eave. Our merchant friend sells these two pounders by the hundreds.

Those who feed birds in town and country have developed ingenious ways of keeping foods safe from unwanted guests. They use nylon mesh bags as pliable and convenient containers for suet, frozen fats, and leftovers. They hang these high—well away from walls or tree trunks. They spike large chunks of suet atop tall posts. These posts, as well as those which support feeding stations, are covered with sheet metal to confound climbers.

The same general principle applies to the placing of the actual feeders. Feeders placed too low, or too close to trees and walls, are fair game for the uninvited. On this point there is division of opinion. Many feeders love birds and animals impartially. They are not averse to squirrels or other four-footers sharing the bounty, reasoning that they are all God's creatures and they too get desperately cold and hungry.

Everyone has his or her own personal approach to bird feeding. We like the birds close for easy viewing and photographing. So we hang feeders and suet balls from our eaves just two feet from our picture window, interspersing them with summer wind chimes.

Bluejays, whiskey jacks, and an occasional hairy woodpecker are too timid for this close approach, so suet in nylon bags is hung from adjacent birches. Occasional kitchen scraps are tossed out on the frozen ground for the jays and squirrels, as well as "unknown" woodland denizens who come to salvage and scavenge in the night.

Every bird variety has personalized characteristics of its very own. Sprightly chickadees are dynamos. They eat from grey dawn to deepest dusk, frantically stoking their tiny bodies against the long nights. Like the hummers which left us in September, they have a natural 110 degree body temperature which requires sufficient fuel to sustain and buttress them against the cruel cold.

Nuthatches are the clowns. They walk headfirst down trees. They eat sideways and upside down, clinging to slippery surfaces with casual ease. At close range we found out why. Their little talons are needle sharp and have an abnormally wide spread. If eagle talons had proportionately wide spreads, they could fly away with houses!

Downy and hairy woodpeckers (the hairy is the big flashy one) like to eat upside down, too. They are rarely at the bird feeders. But they work on the suet balls steadily. They have the strange ability to use their tails as third legs, clamping them to rounded surfaces to hold them steady.

The grosbeaks (mostly the brilliant evening grosbeaks which come at any hour of the day) are the favorites of many, although we have a friend who,

Squirrel-frustrators (left) for those who want to keep furry marauders away from feeders: the inverted trash can cover. Above, a feeder that combines simplicity and capacity—for do-it-yourselfers.

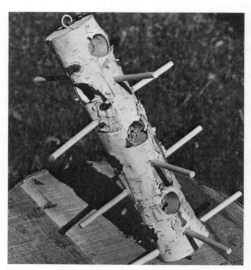

A six-inch birch log, with one and one-half inch holes, three to a side, add a few dowels — and the watcher has a peanut-butter log. This is popular with chickadees, nuthatches, downy and hairy woodpeckers.

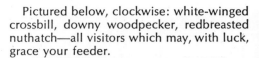

Pictured below, clockwise: white-winged crossbill, downy woodpecker, redbreasted nuthatch—all visitors which may, with luck, grace your feeder.

Helpful guide for the family: "Birds of North America," by Robbins, Brunn, Zim, and Singer. Add good binoculars for closeups. Above left to right: hoary redpoll, American goldfinch (changes to olive-drab coat in winter), cardinal, evening grosbeak, whitebreasted nuthatch.

in the absence of our many rustic kinds, finds pleasure in feeding sparrows and savoring the drama in their lives.

It is the grosbeaks which make heavy inroads on the sunflower seeds. Their powerful, short beaks shuck the seeds in nothing flat. And a steady stream of seed shells dribble from their mouths as they feed. Unlike other birds (which spend most of their time with us) the grosbeaks are travellers. They drop in on us in flocks of six to a dozen, feeding, then leaving to look for goodies on neighbors' shelves. At least we deduce this from the fact that they sometimes show up just once or twice a day—and at other times "slight us" for a full day at a time. The same might be said of those gypsies called red crossbills—vagabonds who may winter with you—and not appear the next year.

Birds are the great common conversation denominator in winter. At times when there isn't much to talk about except the weather, depth of snow, and the common cold, the conversation never lags for the feeding fraternity—and there is always the chance of a rare guest—a shrike or a tufted titmouse, for example.

The man who feeds birds need not and doesn't feel self conscious about this tender side of his life. After

all, there's the touch of the softy in all of us. We've often found that the crudest lout of a man becomes a sweet fellow when watching birds feed at familiar feeders.

So the nights grow longer and temperatures more frigid. It's time for bird feeders to remember that our winter friends live from hour to hour with scant body reserves.

Conscientious bird lovers considerately fill their feeders or have neighbors do for them when they are away. Those who leave for the winter have a special obligation to cooperate with friends and neighbors so that their bird chums aren't suddenly stranded —with no food supply.

The true keynote in bird feeding lies in the character rather than the brains or pedigree of the feeder. This is just another dimension in compassion wherein warm hearts and faithfulness are superior to the irresolute and scattered application of genius and expertise.

So, if you qualify and want to join these growing ranks, get going on your personal feeders. Don't wait until you see the birds. Get the feed out. The birds will come to you!

Volume I - 1931

Volume II - 1932

Volume III - 1933

Volume IV - 1934

Volume V - 1935

Volume VI - 1936

Volume VII - 1937

Volume VIII - 1938

Volume IX - 1939

Volume X - 1940

Volume XI - 1941

Volume XII - 1942

Volume XIII - 1943

Volume XIV - 1944

Volume XV - 1945

Volume XVI - 1946

Volume XVII - 1947

Volume XVIII - 1948

christmas

Christmas 1974 explores the wonder and excitement of the Christmas season in this 44th volume, edited by Randolph E. Haugan, the founder of *Christmas*. Through poems, stories, music, and art we again celebrate the birth of the Savior. The type is set in Linotype Caledonia. Headings are set in Monotype Goudy Blackletter with Lombardic initials. *Christmas* is printed by photo-offset lithography and published by Augsburg Publishing House, Minneapolis, Minnesota.

Volume XIX - 1949

Volume XX - 1950

Volume XXI - 1951

Volume XXII - 1952

Volume XXIII - 1953

Volume XXIV - 1954

Volume XXV - 1955

Volume XXVI - 1956

Volume XXVII - 1957

Volume XXVIII - 1958

Volume XXIX - 1959

Volume XXX - 1960

Volume XXXI - 1961

Volume XXXII - 1962

Volume XXXIII - 1963

Volume XXXIV - 1964

Volume XXXV - 1965

Volume XXXVI - 1966

Volume XXXVII - 1967

Volume XXXVIII - 1968

Volume XXXIX - 1969

Volume XL - 1970

Volume XLI - 1971

Volume XLII - 1972

Volume XLIII - 1973